2025
vision board
CLIP ART BOOK
with Reflection Questions

KALISHIA WINSTON

🎁 YOUR FREE GIFTS

As a token of appreciation for your purchase, I'm excited to offer you four valuable bonuses:

#1: "Creating Your Dream Life with Your Own Vision Board" (Course)

Unlock the potential within you and start manifesting your aspirations with my exclusive vision board course. Set clear intentions and turn your dreams into reality.

#2: "86 Quick & Easy Strategies for Saving Money" (eBook)

Discover 86 practical and easy-to-implement strategies to save money, budget wisely, and achieve your financial goals. This eBook is an indispensable guide for securing your financial future.

#3: "Teach Your Kids to Create Their Future with a Vision Board" (eBook)

Ideal for parents and mentors, this eBook provides essential techniques for teaching family members the power of vision boarding. It is designed to guide adults in fostering goal-setting and visualization skills in children.

To access the first three gifts, sign up for my email newsletter for instant access at gifts2025.kalishiawinston.com. Alongside these gifts, you will also receive tips, free book giveaways, discounts, and so much more.

#4 "2025 Vision Board Clip Art Book" (Printable PDF)

Inside the 2025 Vision Board Clip Art Book, you'll find a treasure trove of inspiring clip art elements to fuel your dreams and creativity. But what if you need extra copies for a vision board party or want to retry cutting out an element? No worries!

Simply enter the link to access the PDF file, ready for printing (no email sign-up required): pdf2025.kalishiawinston.com

All of these bonuses are completely free and come with no strings attached. For the first three gifts, you only need to provide your email address. Enjoy your free gifts, and here's to nurturing dreams and achieving personal goals!

REFLECT AND ENVISION
Guiding Questions for Your Journey

As you embark on creating your vision board, it's important to think deeply about who you are, where you want to go, and what you want to achieve. These reflection questions are designed to inspire you and guide your vision board creation process. Take some time to journal your answers or simply ponder these questions to gain clarity and focus.

Who You Are and What You Value

1. What makes you feel the most empowered and why?
2. Describe a day in your life five years from now. What does it look like?
3. What are three things you love about yourself?
4. What hobbies or activities make you lose track of time?
5. Who do you look up to, and what qualities do they have that you admire?

Facing Fears and Embracing Growth

6. If fear was not a factor, what would you try today?
7. What are you most grateful for in your life right now?
8. What are your top three priorities in life at this moment?
9. How can you make a positive impact on your community?
10. What does success mean to you?

Setting Goals and Dreaming Big

11. What are three goals you have for this year?
12. What qualities do you want to be known for?
13. If you could change one thing about the world, what would it be?
14. What are you most passionate about? How can you do more of that?
15. What does your ideal friendship or relationship look like?

Leveraging Strengths and Overcoming Challenges

16. What are your biggest strengths, and how can you use them more?
17. What is something new you'd like to learn or try out?
18. How do you handle setbacks and challenges?
19. When do you feel the most confident?
20. What does a balanced life look like to you, and how can you achieve it?

Feel free to return to these questions as often as you like. They can serve as a powerful tool to remind you of your strengths, dreams, and the path you are paving for yourself. Each time you revisit them, you might find your answers change as you grow and evolve.

Enjoy the process of discovery, and let these questions guide you as you create a vision board that truly reflects your dreams and aspirations.

New year's resolutions

1
2
3
4
5

CHANGES COMING IN 2025

2025

NEW YEAR

NEW LIFE

NEW YEAR NEW START

TOP PRIORITIES

THINGS TO LEARN

PLACES TO TRAVEL

RESTAURANTS TO VISIT

SKILLS TO DEVELOP

FOODS TO TRY

THINGS TO ACCOMPLISH

BOOKS TO READ

Mind
Body
Soul

FINDING
BALANCE

Meditation

INHALE
EXHALE

KEEP
CALM

CHAKRA

YOGA

HEALTHY START INTO THE NEW YEAR

STAY ACTIVE

BE STRONGER THAN YOUR EXCUSES

FITNESS AT HOME

WORKOUT

PROGRESS

RUNNING

WORRY LESS
RUN MORE

2025

GET FIT!

5K

10K

15K

21K

42K

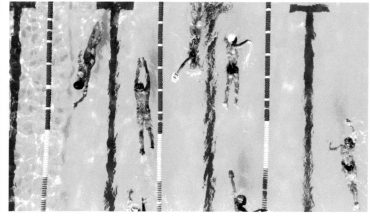

YOUR ONLY
LIMIT IS
YOU

FIND
YOUR
FIRE

A LITTLE
PROGRESS
EACH DAY
ADDS UP
TO BIG
RESULTS

WALK
10000
steps
every
DAY

SWEAT
SMILE
REPEAT

SURF GOLF TENNIS

VOLLEYBALL KARATE JUDO

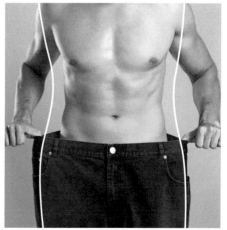

NO POSTING
NO LIKING
JUST LIVING

HOME

SELF CARE
♡

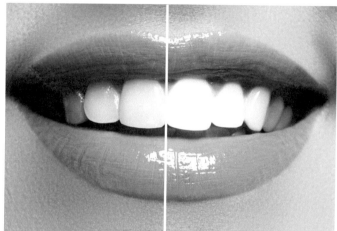

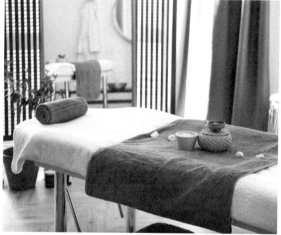

MEN NEED
SELF CARE
TOO

GET ENOUGH
SLEEP

MAKE yourself A PRIORITY

HEALTHY TEETH

Don't forget to love yourself

LEARN A NEW LANGUAGE

ONLINE EDUCATION

Read More Books

GRADUAT²⁰²⁵ON

STUDY

NEW SKILLS

LEARN SOMETHING NEW EVERYDAY

You are NEVER TOO OLD TO learn

audio book

CERTIFICATE

OF ACHIEVEMENT

PROUDLY PRESENTED TO

in recognition of

SIGNATURE

Date

BOSS **LEADER** **MANAGER**

FOUNDER **CEO** **DIRECTOR**

build your own empire

GIRLBOSS

Come in WE'RE OPEN

BUSINESS PLAN

Delegate

WORK FROM HOME

Debt Free!

PASSIVE INCOME

No IMPULSE BUYING

My bank account **grows** every day.

SAVINGS GOAL

Create MULTIPLE Streams OF INCOME

EMERGENCY FUND

Create a Diverse Portfolio Of Investments

REAL ESTATE

MAKE MONEY INVEST IT AND MAKE MORE.

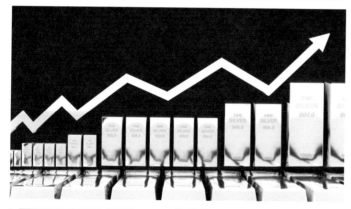

Retirement Plan

ROI

RETURN ON INVESTMENT

Cryptocurrency

INVEST IN Yourself

Business Angel

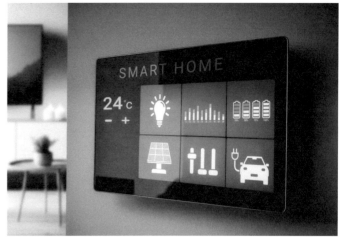

PENTHOUSE DREAMHOME

DREAM CAR DRIVER LICENSE

GARDENING

PHOTOGRAPHY

PAINTING

KNITTING

WOODWORKING

POTTERY

COOKING

BAKING

DRAWING

WRITING

PLAYING GUITAR

SINGING

PIANO PLAYING

DIY PROJECTS

JOURNALING

BLOGGING

BIRD WATCHING

FISHING

ASTRONOMY

DANCING

DIGITAL ART

PODCASTING

SCRAPBOOKING

MODEL BUILDING

BOARD GAMES

UPCYCLING

LOVE IS LOVE

Find Love

Date Night

STRONGER
together

SHE SAID *Yaaasss!* ♡ — *engaged*

≫≫ honeymoon → ♥ together forever ♥

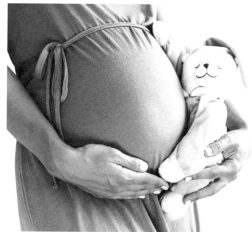

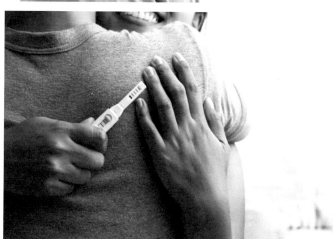

baby

shower

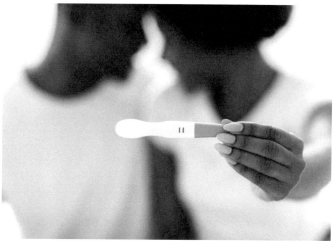

BABY IS COMING

coming soon...

it's a BOY

it's a GIRL

time spent with *family* is worth *every second*

BEST MOM EVER

BEST DAD EVER

In laughter, and in tears, always together.

FRIEND♥SHIP UNBREAKABLEBOND

KEEP DONATE

LIVE WITH LESS CLUTTER

LESS STUFF MORE HAPPINESS

BUY LESS CHOOSE WELL

simplicity over clutter

Get Organized

BLOOD **DONATION** **SAVE LIFE**

Giving Back Feels Good

MAKE A DIFFERENCE

Spread kindness

ADOPT

HEALTHY PETS
happy life

ADVENTURE EXPLORE MORE

GO GREEN

Reduce

Reuse   Recycle

ZERO WASTE   ECO-FRIENDLY

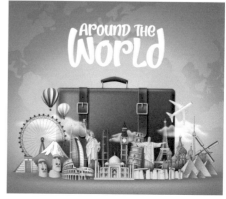

LUXURY
LIVING

WEALTH
BUILDING

PARIS	ROME	LONDON
TOKYO	SYDNEY	BARCELONA
VENICE	DUBAI	BANGKOK
NEW YORK CITY	LOS ANGELES	SAN FRANCISCO
LAS VEGAS	MIAMI	ORLANDO
HONOLULU	CHICAGO	NEW ORLEANS
WASHINGTON, D.C.	NASHVILLE	SEATTLE
AUSTIN	PHILADELPHIA	BOSTON
ATLANTA	SAN DIEGO	GRAND CANYON
YELLOWSTONE NATIONAL PARK	YOSEMITE NATIONAL PARK	NIAGARA FALLS
TORONTO	VANCOUVER	MONTREAL
BANFF NATIONAL PARK	CANCUN	TULUM
MEXICO CITY	CABO SAN LUCAS	PLAYA DEL CARMEN

PUNTA CANA	SAN JUAN	HAVANA
RIO DE JANEIRO	BUENOS AIRES	LIMA
MACHU PICCHU	SANTIAGO	BOGOTA
NICE	AMSTERDAM	BERLIN
MUNICH	VIENNA	PRAGUE
BUDAPEST	ISTANBUL	ATHENS
SANTORINI	MYKONOS	COPENHAGEN
STOCKHOLM	OSLO	HELSINKI
REYKJAVIK	ZURICH	GENEVA
LISBON	MADRID	SEVILLE
MILAN	FLORENCE	NAPLES
CAPE TOWN	MARRAKECH	CAIRO
SINGAPORE	HONG KONG	BALI

I am rich IN ALL AREAS OF MY LIFE

GRATEFUL FOR where I am EXCITED ABOUT where I am going

I attract wonderful people into my life

I AM RICH WITH OPPORTUNITIES to achieve my goals.

Dream big SET GOALS TAKE ACTION

MY FINANCIAL SUCCESS ALLOWS ME TO LIVE A LIFE OF ABUNDANCE AND SHARE WITH THOSE IN NEED.

Create a life YOU CAN'T WAIT TO WAKE UP TO.

WHATEVER YOU DECIDE TO DO MAKE SURE IT MAKES YOU Happy

Be your OWN INSPIRATION

Success DOESN'T COME FROM WHAT YOU DO OCCASIONALLY. IT COMES FROM WHAT YOU DO CONSISTENTLY.

Look for something positive IN EACH DAY, EVEN IF SOME DAYS YOU HAVE TO LOOK a little harder.

I am creating the life of my dreams.

BIG DREAMS HAVE SMALL BEGINNINGS.

Your future DEPENDS ON MANY THINGS BUT MOSTLY ON YOU.

I am WORTH OVER A MILLION DOLLARS.

BANK *of* ABUNDANCE

MAKE IT HAPPEN

For manifesting purposes only.

Pay to the order of _____

$

_____

DOLLARS

Note _____

Date _____

_____
Signature

BOARDING PASS

BOARDING PASS TO .....

NAME:

TIME: DATE:

ADDRESS:

FOR MANIFESTING PURPOSES ONLY.

NAME OF PASSENGER

DESTINATION

DATE

FLIGHT CLASS SEAT

Cruise

YOUR BOARDING PASS

A special ticket for a special person

PASSENGER NAME

DESTINATION

DEPART ON   PORT

FOR MANIFESTING PURPOSES ONLY.

ADMIT ONE

YOU'RE GOING TO
....

....

DATE   VENUE   TIME

FOR MANIFESTING PURPOSES ONLY.

ADMIT ONE

DREAMS	LOVE	HAPPINESS
HEALTH	WEALTH	TRAVEL
FITNESS	CAREER	EDUCATION
HOME	FAMILY	FRIENDS
PASSION	SAVINGS	ASSETS
PEACE	STRENGTH	SUCCESS
JOURNEY	GROWTH	HARMONY
BALANCE	PATIENCE	GRATITUDE
INSPIRE	RESILIENCE	HOBBY
JOY	CREATIVITY	CHANGE
COURAGE	TRUST	LEADER
FOCUS	EMPATHY	SECURITY
CHARITY	SELF-LOVE	FREEDOM
SIMPLICITY	WELLBEING	KINDNESS

UNLOCK MORE INSPIRATION!

Thank you for choosing the **2025 Vision Board Clip Art Book** as your tool for visualizing your dreams and goals. To offer even more inspiration, I'm excited to provide you with free downloadable PDFs of my previous books, the **2023 Vision Board Clip Art Book** and the **2024 Vision Board Clip Art Book**. These resources will give you access to additional images, quotes, and ideas to enhance your vision board.

 ## Download Your Free PDFs:

- Simply scan the QR code below or enter the link to access the downloads. Choose the pages that resonate with you and print them at home or at your local print shop for even more images and inspiration.

 **pdfs.kalishiawinston.com**

 ## Explore More of My Work:

If you've enjoyed this book, I invite you to explore all of my other books available on Amazon. Each book is designed to inspire and motivate you on your journey toward achieving your goals.

- Scan the QR code below or visit the link to browse and discover more of my inspiring collections.

 **amazon.com/stores/author/B0BB89HSM3**

 ## Share Your Experience:

Your thoughts matter! Please consider leaving an honest review on Amazon. Your feedback helps others discover the perfect tool for their vision board journey.

 ## Recommend to Friends:

If you know someone who might benefit from this book, please feel free to recommend it. Sharing inspiration with friends can help them unlock their potential and achieve their dreams as well.

Thank you for being part of this journey. May your vision board help you turn your dreams into reality. Happy creating!

Made in the USA
Columbia, SC
05 January 2025

51296784R00046